Summary of

The Old Man and the Sea

by Ernest Hemingway

Written by Neil Parker

The Old Man and the Sea– Summary

Santiago is an old fisherman located in Cuba. He has not caught a single fish in more than eighty-four days. Santiago is thin with many wrinkles on his neck and scars on his hands from carrying heavy fish. He also has cheerful eyes, no matter his lack of success. He doesn't let this unsuccessfulness destroy his spirit though. Santiago doesn't have many friends and his only friend is a little boy named Manolin. Manolin helped on Santiago's boat during the unsuccessful first forty days of no catches. However, after those forty days, Manolin's parents said that Santiago was unlucky and moved him to another boat, but he still helps bring the empty boat for Santiago every day he can.

Manolin had made some money on the successful boat so he asked Santiago if he can come back to working with him. Santiago, however, tells him to listen to his parents and to stay with the boat that is making him money. Confiding in the little boy, Santiago tells him his big plan to go farther out into the Gulf to try fishing there. Manolin promises that he will try to convince his new boss to go fishing out towards where Santiago will be, so they can help in any way if he so happens to need it. All of a sudden, Manolin offers to get some sardines for him, and Santiago refuses but then later accepts the kind offer.

Manolin and Santiago grab things from the boat and head towards Santiago's house, which resembles a shed. The house contained a bed, table, chair, religious portraits, a picture of his wife, and a dirt floor. Nothing special about it but in fact something very simple that worked for the old man. The picture of Santiago's wife had been taken down, however, because it caused him to become very lonely and depressed with looking at it. At the house, Santiago and Manolin begin the nightly ritual of talking about rice, fish and a cast net that had been sold ages ago. The little boy talks about getting the sardines for dinner, but Santiago pulls out a piece of paper, where they then begin talking of baseball and Joe DiMaggio. He tells the boy to trust in the Yankees and DiMaggio, that they will pull through. Santiago tells the little boy that since tomorrow is the eighty-fifth day that he hasn't caught a fish, and since that eighty-five is quite a lucky number, he's been thinking of buying a lottery ticket with that number on it. Manolin leaves and Santiago takes a nap.

Manolin arrives back to Santiago's house and wakes the old man. The little boy has brought them dinner, so they eat together. Manolin realizes that Santiago isn't living the greatest and tells himself to remember to bring the old man a new shirt, jacket, shoes, and a blanket before winter hits. They talk of baseball again, focusing mainly on Joe DiMaggio. Since they were talking about the greatest baseball stars, a fleeting thought crosses Manolin's mind and he mutters out that Santiago is the greatest fisherman. The old man accepts the compliment but then tells Manolin that his statement isn't true because he knew men who were much greater fishermen than he is. Manolin takes his leave for the night and Santiago goes back to sleep.

That night, Santiago dreamed of traveling to Africa as a shipmate. In Africa, he lived on the beach listening to the surf roll in and out, watching native boats floating through it. Then, his dream turned to different places; to lions that were roaming on the beach. Santiago wakes up in the morning and heads to Manolin's house to get him. They then take Santiago's supplies from his house and head to his boat. Once arriving there, the little boy heads to get some sardines and when he returns, he wishes Santiago luck. Santiago leaves, headed out to sea in the early morning.

After a few moments, Santiago rowed over a pit that dropped to over four thousand feet. It was here that shrimp, squid, and baitfish liked to hang out and congregate. After moving along, he saw flying fish and birds that were overjoyed with the gathering shrimp, squid and baitfish. Santiago has a crossing thought, he wonders why birds were made in such a delicate matter, but the ocean was kind and beautiful; but quite cruel at the same time. Santiago was the only fisherman who considered the ocean to be feminine, and the other fisherman considered the ocean an enemy and competitor.

Santiago continues on, way past the spot that he was usually fishing at but was not able to catch any fish. He travels past the schools of albacore and bonito, stopping just before leaving their swimming grounds. He hopes to himself that there is a bigger fish amongst the group of fish. Santiago gets his line ready and casts it out but not allowing it to follow the current. Instead letting it go to certain spots that he wanted it too. Talking to himself, Santiago tells the air around him that every day is a brand-new day and that just because he doesn't have any luck, that could change. He then admits to rather wanting to be exact on his actions and then whenever luck finally came; he would be ready.

Santiago spies a man-of-war bird flying above him searching and then spying something located in the water. He follows the bird, letting his cast down in the areas the bird was watching. He had his hopes up that he would catch a bigger fish and he looks around, waiting. There's a group of dolphins swimming past but going way too fast for either Santiago or even the bird to catch. So, he moves on wondering if he'll catch a marlin that could be tracking the school of fish. Suddenly, a Portuguese man-of-war comes up to the boat and Santiago remembers being stung by one of them. To him, the tops of the jellyfish were beautiful enough to want to touch but they contained a false meaning, and they were one of the fakest things in the ocean. Santiago took joy in watching the larger sea turtles bite into them, swallowing them whole. He also contains a large amount of empathy towards turtles because they are extremely strong. Everything about them resembles being strong. If you cut a turtle up, their heart would still keep on beating. Santiago then compares himself to the turtles.

    Noticing the bird once again, Santiago suspects that the bird actually found something. Shortly after, a tuna leaps out of the water and the bird takes a dive for the bait- fish that started to panic because of the splash the tuna made. Gently moving more toward the school of fish, he eventually gets a bite on his line. Santiago pulls the cast in along with an albacore hanging from the end. He quickly beats it until it's no longer breathing. The old man realizes that he is breaking a virtue of the sea. This virtue was talking way too much while out at sea. Santiago has always respected this virtue, and since he has recently been talking aloud quite often, he realizes that he has to focus on one thought alone. His job as a fisherman, the one thing that he was born to do.

All of a sudden, Santiago's fishing pole bends sharply letting him know that he has a bite and he notices it's a pretty hard bite with the way his pole was bending. The next tug that came was a bit harder than the first, and at this moment, Santiago knows that it's the marlin. Nibbling a bit more but not quite taking the full bait, Santiago talks to the fish as if trying to get him to take the entire baitfish. He coaxes the fish not to be shy, to go ahead and eat the bait fish so that he could have a nice cold tuna. After a few fake bites, the marlin finally takes a bite out of the tuna along with quite a bit of the fishing line. Santiago waits a few moments before he uses as much strength he has to pull in the line and to bring the marlin to the surface.

The marlin is extremely strong and doesn't emerge on the surface like Santiago was hoping, but instead, begins swimming away. The marlin was still attached to the fishing line, so he ended up dragging Santiago and his boat through the water. A fleeting thought of wishing Manolin was with him to help crossed Santiago's mind. He realizes that he has to let the marlin take as much of the fishing line he wants, or he'll lose it. The marlin will get tired eventually, at least this was what Santiago thought. The marlin kept swimming for four hours straight while the old man was braced against the boat.

    The sun starts to set, and the marlin is still swimming onward. Santiago looks back to see how far land was from him and he notices that he cannot see any, as if land didn't exist and the sea was the only thing in the world. He thinks back to when the boy helped him with fishing in the past and wishes that he was with him now. He has a passing thought of that the older you get, the more you should have a companion but that there is also nothing stopping you from being alone. A couple of porpoises stick their heads out of the water and Santiago speaks aloud, saying that they love one another. Remembering a time when he and Manolin had caught a female marlin and the male stayed by the boat, swimming about and jumping out of the water in despair just to be able to see his mate. Santiago remarks saying that it was the saddest thing he had seen in his entire life.

    Behind Santiago, the line bends letting him know that he got a bite. He quickly cuts the line and wishes that Manolin was there with him to watch his other lines. He tells the marlin that he isn't letting him go and will be staying with him until he dies. Santiago doesn't know if he'd want to have the fish jump, so their struggle is over. However, he also worries that if the fish does such a thing, the hook will come loose and then he would not catch the marlin. He tells the marlin that he loves him but that he will also be dead by the end of the day. A bird lands on the side of the boat and Santiago asks it it's age and then begins worrying about the safety of the bird since there were hawks that could swipe it up and kill it.

While Santiago speaks to the bird as if it's an old friend, the marlin pulls on the line which yanks the boat forward causing the old man to cut his hand. He washes it in the water and notices that the marlin is starting to finally slow down. Grabbing a tuna, he begins cutting the fish, so he can eat it to regain his strength. Santiago's left hand begins to cramp, and he becomes a bit frustrated, saying that even if his hand turned into a claw, it wouldn't do any good. He quickly eats the tuna and then sits and waits, wondering about the situation he is in.

Santiago looks around him at the endless depth of water, then looking up he stares at the clouds. He notices a flock of geese flying above, going in and out of the covering of clouds that litter the sky. He has a fleeting thought that a man is never actually alone when out on the sea. Looking down at his hand, Santiago thinks about how cramps are an act of humiliation against their own body. A splash sounds, Santiago takes notice of the marlin jumping out of the water and then back in. He becomes amazed at the sight of the marlin and he realizes that the size of the marlin could destroy the boat if it so happened to want too. Santiago quickly sends a prayer to calm his worrying heart, and he settles into catching the marlin once again.

    Unsure of how much longer he would be chasing the marlin, he casts another line to catch some food, so that he can gain some strength. His injured hand stops cramping and begins to relax. Santiago's mind goes to Joe DiMaggio and how he has a bone spur, he concludes that men and beast are no different. The sun begins setting, while he thinks about his past hoping it would gain him confidence in his situation now. He remembers when he was in an arm-wrestling match located in Casablanca. It had lasted for an entire day and night but he, El Campeon as he was known then, won eventually.

    Santiago's food fishing line bobs and he pulls it in quickly, revealing that he caught a dolphin fish right before it became dark out.

Taking the fish off the line, he throws it back out just in the off chance that he has to eat again to regain strength. The sun begins setting and Santiago ties his boat's oars together, so they create more of a drag against the still moving marlin. Once he finished with that task, he looked up at the stars and began communicating with them. He considers them his friends alongside the marlin and admits that he's never seen a fish like him, but he has to kill the marlin. He then tells the stars that he's quite glad that he and other humans don't have to kill the beautiful stars. Thinking back on what he just said, he realizes that he actually truly feels sorry for the marlin and comes to the conclusion that the people that would buy his meat at the market, are not worthy of eating the meat from such a noble beast.

    Santiago then realizes that he is utterly exhausted. He decides to get some shut-eye before he can actually kill the marlin. To prevent the dolphin fish that he had caught earlier from spoiling, he cuts it open and cleans it. Taking a few bites, he tries to make himself comfortable, so that he can sleep. Wrapping the line around his body and touching the rope, which the marlin was attached too, with his right hand. He leaned against the bow and shut his eyes. Quickly, he was sound asleep and began to dream of schools of fish. More importantly, porpoises; like the two that he had seen earlier in the day. His dream changes to his village home and in this dream, his right arm is asleep. Although in reality, it is actually awake because it is on the rope, so he can be ready when the marlin lurches forwards. Finally, his dream turns to the lions on the African beach, this was a recurring dream back in his younger days, and he gets an overjoyed feeling across his body.

Santiago is jerked awake with a burning sensation in his right hand and realizes that the line is being dragged in a rather frantic motion through his hand. The marlin leaps up out of the water and Santiago quickly holds onto the line, so he doesn't lose the fish. This line though has caused his hand to become cut, and his left hand is no use because it is still asleep. This makes it hard to hold onto the line with just one hand that was quickly becoming almost to its breaking point. He quickly gained his balance and a realization crossed his mind. Since the marlin leaped out of the water, it's air sacks were now full, which prevented him from diving any deeper than what he was at. He kept trying too because he wanted to die in peace, deep within the water. Marlin leaps out of the water once more and Santiago wipes raw dolphin meat off his face since he didn't want to lose his stomach and his strength. He needed everything he had to fight the marlin.

When the sun started to rise, the marlin began circling. Santiago held onto the rope as tight as he could, trying desperately to pull the line in as slowly as he can without the marlin noticing. He talks to himself, saying that with each pull he does, it'll slowly bring the marlin to him within an hour notice, then he can convince the marlin to allow him to kill him. All of a sudden, Santiago starts to feel faint and begins to worry that he will not win in this long and treacherous fight that he has been in with the marlin. He sends a quick prayer to God saying that he will say all the prayers he knows later, only if he can get the strength to defeat the marlin now.

Santiago continues to slowly pull on the line, but the marlin ends up catching the line with its spear and gains some of the line back. Once the marlin is clear again, Santiago retrieves all of the line that he had just lost. The marlin makes a third turn and Santiago sees the fish for the very first time. He marvels at its size and then gets the harpoon ready while still pulling on the line. The marlin tries to pull away, but Santiago doesn't allow it. Unable to speak due to dehydration, in his mind he says "You are killing me, fish... But you have a right too. Never have I seen a greater, or more beautiful, or a calmer or more noble thing than you, brother. Come on and kill me. I do not care who kills who."

The marlin continues to circle, getting closer and closer to Santiago but then pulling away last minute. Finally, the marlin is close enough that he is quickly harpooned in the chest. The fish quickly leapt out of the water one last time to show its beauty and great length, then falls back to the water belly up in a pool of red water. Santiago gazes for a moment at his prize and then begins the hard work of getting the fish somehow onto land. Santiago realizes that the fish is too heavy to be put on the boat, so he ties it to the skiff. Once the marlin is secured alongside Santiago's boat, Santiago draws the sail and begins the trek southwest towards his home.

After about an hour, a Mako shark pops up. It followed the trail of blood that the marlin was leaving. Coming towards the boat, Santiago grabs the harpoon and prepares to kill the shark before it got to the marlin. All of a sudden, the sharks head and back were out of the water, and Santiago flung the harpoon into its head. Sinking to the bottom of the ocean, Santiago looks at the damage that the shark had caused. He realizes that the shark had taken a good forty or so pounds out of the perfect side of the marlin. Now, Santiago doesn't like the sight of the marlin. He takes the mutilated marlin side as a hit to himself, his ego and his confidence. Regret begins to form within Santiago, and he starts wishing that this long adventure was nothing but a terrible dream. He then comes to the conclusion that man cannot be defeated, only destroyed.

Santiago begins to think about the killing of the marlin, was it a sin? He comes to the conclusion that if killing the marlin to feed himself and others is a sin, then everything else in life is also a sin. He quickly realizes that he didn't just kill the marlin for food, but also for his pride and because he is a fisherman. He loved the fish before, during, and after killing it; not making it a sin. Santiago stops concentrating on his thoughts but instead, getting back to shore. Eating some of the fish, he makes a mental note on how delicious the marlin tastes. After another two hours, two more sharks arrived. But this time, Santiago's harpoon was at the bottom of the ocean in the head of the Mako shark. He takes his knife and fastens it to the end of the oar. Using this, he kills the first shark but didn't have luck with the second.

The second shark shakes the boat as it begins to eat the marlin from within the water. Santiago apologizes to the dead fish and admits that he messed up for going out so far. By now, he has grown tired and has begun to lose his sense of hope. He sits and waits for the next attack to come and sure enough, a single shovel-nosed shark arrived. Santiago kills it but breaks off the knife from the oar. The sun begins to set, and more sharks arrive, but now, he only has a club to defend himself and the marlin with. He isn't able to kill these new sharks but is able to injure them enough that they stay away. Santiago begins to look forward to when night hits; then he would be able to see the lights of Havana.

Ten o'clock rolls around and the lights of Havana shine for Santiago. He begins headed there when a pack of sharks arrive. This time, Santiago knows that fighting with them is useless because he can only see the faint lines their fins make in the water. Desperately, he tries to beat them away from marlin but shortly after he began, one of the sharks took the club. Santiago quickly grabs the tiller and attacks until that too was broken. The last shark in the pack leaves and Santiago begins to sail towards Havana. Now, he is sailing much lighter and he had no feelings or thoughts for the now useless adventure he went on. Concentrating on getting home, he ignores the next pack of sharks that come to gnaw on the marlin's bones. Blood polls in Santiago's mouth and he spits it into the ocean, cursing the sharks at the same time.

Arriving on the shore, he realizes that everyone is asleep. He steps out of his boat, carrying his mast with him to his shack. Falling down, he laid there for a while before he tried to get back up. It becomes too difficult to get up, so he sits for a few moments more while looking at the road. Finally, Santiago is able to get up, but he has to stop quite a few more times before he reaches his home. Once there, he crawls into bed and falls asleep instantly.

In the morning, Manolin arrives at Santiago's shack. He enters and realizes that Santiago is still asleep, so he leaves to get some coffee. While walking and crying along the road to the Terrace, he sees a gathering of fishermen around Santiago's skiff. He goes up to it and sees the men measuring the marlin. Manolin then returns to Santiago's shack and enters. Now, Santiago is up, and the man and boy talk for a while. Manolin then speaks up about how the both of them will be fishing together again but Santiago denies him, saying that he is unlucky. Manolin tells Santiago that he will bring the luck and the old man accepts this while Manolin leaves to get food. That afternoon, a female tourist noticed the skeleton of the marlin and asks the waiter what kind of fish it was. Not a native English speaker, the waiter responds with "shark." She turns to her partner and tells him that she didn't know that sharks had exquisite tails. While this was going, Santiago was still in his shack face down, sleeping and dreaming of lions while Manolin sat by his side and watched him.

Major Themes

<u>Unity:</u> Hemingway makes many connections between Santiago and the natural environment. There are also elements that are contradictory with one another such as the sea is kind yet cruel and both feminine and masculine. Success and failure are both equal faces for Santiago and they come and go, never affecting the unity between him and nature. If he focuses on this unity, he cannot be defeated.

<u>Heroism:</u> The vision that Hemingway has for heroism requires labor that is continuous for the passing ends to come. The hero has to face adversity with not only grace but dignity as well and no matter whether they fail or achieve, internally we still are noble to ourselves.

<u>Manhood:</u> Hemingway's ideal man is one who behaves with dignity and honor, accepting of their duty and to have a maximum amount of self-control. Santiago tells himself to "suffer like a man" because this shows the reader how to live a life like a man and also heroically.

Pride: A hero must have pride interwoven throughout his actions. Santiago travels further across the sea to catch the marlin than any other human being has travelled because of his pride. He also admits of murdering the marlin, also referred to as brother by Santiago, because of his pride. Some think that the loss of the marlin is also as a price for Santiago since he had to travel so far. While others think that his pride is what gave him a great challenge. Pride is a positive trait to have, especially with it interwoven into a job.

Success: There are outer, material success and inner, spiritual success that Hemingway draws upon. Santiago doesn't have outer, material success. This is because he became undefeated at the end of the novel due to the fact that he had to give up his most valuable possession.

Worthiness: To demonstrate being a hero and also a man, you must also have dignity. Santiago is obsessed in trying to prove his worth, which he proved to the boy and to the marlin. But one thing most forget, to have inner peace you must have a constant revolving demonstration of noble actions which will, in turn, prove your worth.

Religion: Manolin shows a devotion to Santiago very similar to that of a religious devotion to church. His father had made him switch boats because it had been 40 days that Santiago's boat had not caught a fish. This correlates to Jesus wandering in the desert being tempted for 40 days by Satan. Santiago doesn't give into his exhaustion when fighting the marlin as Jesus didn't give into temptation.

Quotes

"Have faith in the Yankees my son. Think of the great Joe DiMaggio." - Speaking of baseball, Santiago shows his admiration for DiMaggio who becomes a symbol of manhood for Santiago. He gains strength in catching Marlin because of DiMaggio's strength.

"There are many good fishermen and some great ones. But there is only you." - Manolin tells Santiago this to describe how he's very similar to DiMaggio. Santiago respects the sea, and this is because of the relationship Santiago and the sea has.

"They are good... They play and make jokes and love one another. They are our brothers like the flying fish." - The porpoises visit when Santiago is feeling lonely. They give him strength by coming as a couple and representing love. To Santiago, they are his brothers as every other creature of the sea is.

"Fish... I'll stay with you until I am dead." - Santiago tells this to the Marlin as a commitment to the task of losing strength and energy trailing the fish.

"Fish... I love you and respect you very much. But I will kill you dead before this day ends." - Santiago talks to the fish as if he was an equal to him; he talks of his commitment to keep working as a fisherman no matter the cost.

"He didn't beat you. Not the fish." - Santiago is talking about the sharks beating him to the fish and talks about betraying the fish by letting the sharks eat the fish.

"I didn't know sharks had such handsome, beautifully formed tails." - A female tourist considers the fish skeleton a shark skeleton because she misheard the waiter. This confusion is a representation of the mast difference in opinions of the average person and the sea creatures along with Santiago's relationship with the sea.

"I am a strange old man." - This is identification of how unique Santiago is and demonstrates the strength of will and body that follows. This also demonstrates how he feels about the sea creatures.

"*Anyone can be a fisherman in May.*" - Being a fisherman has its hardships, like being outside in the cold trying to make a living but Santiago see's it more as a challenge. Throughout the book, Santiago will struggle with trying to make a living catching fish, but he does not have anything else he can do. He succeeds in his own determination, even when he isn't successful.

"*If sharks come, God pity him and me.*" - Santiago is determined to not be worthless. This quote is a foreshadowing of the sharks that will come to eat the meat of the marlin. Implying that the marlin and Santiago are one in one another.

Characters

Santiago: The protagonist. An old fisherman who lives in Cuba. He represents Hemingway in a way, searching for the next thing in life. A hero in the face of tragedy.

Manolin: Only friend Santiago has, also a close companion to him. Acts as a surrogate for the reader.

The Marlin: Plays an important role in the book. This is the fish that Santiago spends majority of his time trying to catch, kill and bring ashore. Santiago idealizes the Marlin.

The Sea: The sea is also a crucial character in the book. Santiago resembles the sea, and he refers to the sea as a woman, representing the femininity within his masculinity.

Made in the USA
Middletown, DE
01 July 2024